NATIONAL
GEOGRAPHIC
School Publishing

The Changing Earth

Nisha Da Silva

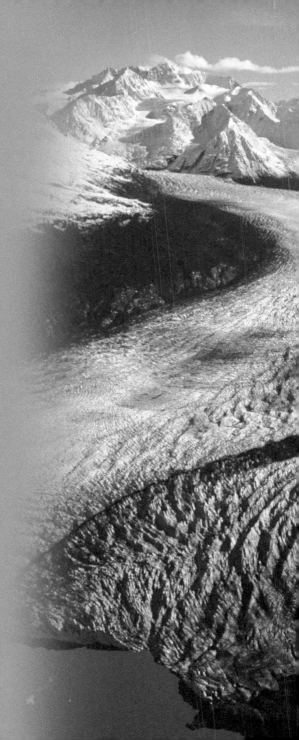

PICTURE CREDITS

Cover, 1, 2, 4–5 (all), 6–7 (all), 9 (left), 10 (left), 12 (all), 13 (right), 14, 15 (left), 16, 17 (left), 18, 19 (left), 20 (left above and left below), 21 (all), Photolibrary.com; 9 (right), 11 (right), 13 (left), 15 (above right), 19 (right), APL/Corbis; 11 (left), Newspix; 17 (right), Getty Images; 20 (right), Pacific Press Service/Alamy.

Produced through the worldwide resources of the National Geographic Society, John M. Fahey, Jr., President and Chief Executive Officer; Gilbert M. Grosvenor, Chairman of the Board; Nina D. Hoffman, Executive Vice President and President, Books and Education Publishing Group.

PREPARED BY NATIONAL GEOGRAPHIC SCHOOL PUBLISHING

Steve Mico, Executive Vice President and Publisher, Children's Books and Education Publishing Group; Marianne Hiland, Editor in Chief; Lynnette Brent, Executive Editor; Michael Murphy and Barbara Wood, Senior Editors; Nicole Rouse, Editor; Bea Jackson, Design Director; David Dumo, Art Director; Shanin Glenn, Designer; Margaret Sidlosky, Illustrations Director; Matt Wascavage, Manager of Publishing Services; Sean Philpotts, Production Manager.

MANUFACTURING AND QUALITY MANAGEMENT

Christopher A. Liedel, Chief Financial Officer; Phillip L. Schlosser, Vice President; Clifton M. Brown III, Director.

BOOK DEVELOPMENT

Ibis for Kids Australia Pty Limited.

Published by the National Geographic Society
1145 17th Street, N.W.
Washington, D.C. 20036-4688

Product No. 4W1005073

ISBN-13: 978-1-4263-5069-6
ISBN-10: 1-4263-5069-4

23 22 21 20 19 18
4 5 6 7 8 9 10 11 12 13 14 15

Printed in USA

Contents

volcano

glacier

earthquake damage

What do you know about natural forces?
How can natural forces change Earth's surface?

waterfall

desert

Earth's Changing Surface

The **surface** of Earth is constantly changing. These changes can happen slowly. They can also happen quickly.

Earth's surface can be changed by wind. In this desert, wind moves sand dunes and wears away rock.

Earth's surface can be changed by water. This river has slowly worn away rock and soil to create a canyon.

A volcano can cause quick changes to Earth's surface. Hot lava and ash pour out and cover the land.

Earth's Moving Crust

Earth is covered by a layer of soil and rock called the crust. Earth's crust is broken into huge pieces called **tectonic plates**. These plates are constantly moving. This movement changes Earth's surface.

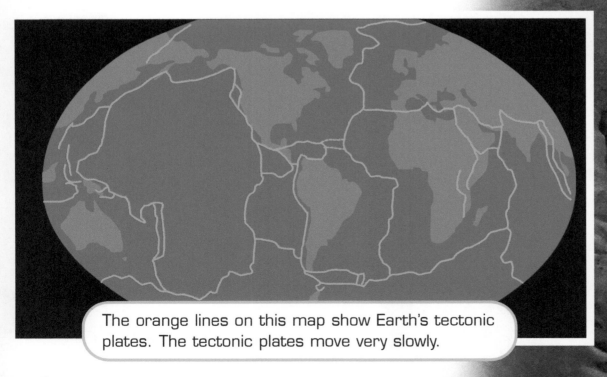

The orange lines on this map show Earth's tectonic plates. The tectonic plates move very slowly.

This picture shows a place where two tectonic plates meet. These plates move sideways against each other. Sometimes this can cause **earthquakes**.

Sometimes tectonic plates move toward each other. This can push Earth's crust up and form mountains.

Earthquakes

Earthquakes can happen when two tectonic plates push against each other and get stuck. Eventually, the rocks at the edges of the plates break. This makes the ground shake.

An earthquake can cause huge changes to Earth's surface. These cracks were formed after an earthquake in Peru.

An earthquake can occur under the sea and cause a huge wave. When the huge wave reaches the shore, it can knock down trees and buildings.

Scientists use the Richter [*RIK-ter*] scale to measure the force of an earthquake. Most people cannot feel an earthquake that measures less than 3 on the Richter scale.

The biggest earthquake ever measured was under the sea near Chile in 1960. It measured 9.5 on the Richter scale and caused a huge wave. This picture shows damage that was caused by the wave.

Volcanoes

In some places, the edges of Earth's tectonic plates are cracked. Hot, melted rock called magma can **erupt** through these cracks. This is how a **volcano** is formed.

As magma comes out of a volcano, it can cool and form dust, ash, and small pieces of rock. Dust clouds from a volcano can be up to 50 miles high.

When magma erupts from a volcano, it is called lava. Lava can flow down the sides of a volcano at up to 30 miles an hour.

Ash and lava from a volcano can cover large areas of land. Over time, the ash and lava change into soil. This soil is very good for growing crops.

Even though there is a chance that some volcanoes may erupt again, there are many farming communities near volcanoes.

As a volcano erupts, ash, dust, and rock can build up around it to form a cone-shaped mountain.

Wind

Wind **erosion** can slowly change the shape of Earth's surface. Wind can also change Earth's surface quickly.

The winds of a **tornado** can spin at up to 300 miles an hour. A powerful tornado can knock down trees and buildings.

Wind can blow sand and soil over hundreds of miles. When the sand and soil land, they cover the ground and change the landscape.

Grains of sand carried by the wind have helped to change the shape of this rock.

Water

Water can change Earth's surface, too. It falls as rain, hail, and snow. It moves in rivers, **glaciers**, and the sea. All of these forms of water can cause changes.

As waves crash against the shore, they carry away tiny pieces of rock. Over a long period of time, the shape of the coastline changes.

Weathering can change the shape of rocks beneath a river. Over time, this can form a canyon.

If a lot of rain falls on a hillside in a short period of time, the soil can become soft and slippery. This can lead to a landslide.

Some parts of Earth are so cold that snow does not melt. As layers of snow build up they turn into ice. Sometimes the layers become so heavy they start to slide. These moving sheets of ice are called glaciers.

As a glacier moves, rocks and soil get caught in the bottom layer of ice. The moving ice, rock, and soil erode the ground underneath the glacier, creating a valley.

Ice from glaciers can crack huge rocks. As the cracks get bigger and bigger, pieces of the rock break away. These mountains were shaped by glaciers.

Did You Know?

Thousands of years ago, the climate on Earth was much colder than it is now. For long periods, much of Earth's surface was covered in ice. These times are known as **ice ages**.

This picture shows the Great Lakes. They fill an area that was carved out by glaciers during the last ice age.

What causes changes to Earth's surface?
Which changes happen quickly?
Which changes happen slowly?

earthquake

erosion

erupt

glacier

ice age

surface

tectonic plate

volcano

weathering

Glossary

earthquake (page 9)

A movement of tectonic plates that makes Earth's surface shake

A violent earthquake can leave huge cracks in Earth's surface.

erosion (page 14)

The movement of soil and worn down rock from one place to another

Erosion can gradually change the shape of a coastline.

erupt (page 12)

To burst out of an opening

When a volcano erupts, it can cause a dust cloud many miles high.

glacier (page 16)

A large, thick, moving mass of ice

A glacier can create a deep valley.

ice age (page 19)

A period of time when Earth was much colder than it is now

The Great Lakes were created by glaciers during the last ice age.

KEY CONCEPT
KEY CONCEPT
KEY CONCEPT
KEY CONCEPT
KEY CONCEPT

surface (page 6)
The top or outer part of something
Wind can change Earth's surface.

tectonic plate (page 8)
A huge section of Earth's crust
Earth's surface is divided into huge pieces called tectonic plates.

tornado (page 14)
A spinning windstorm
A tornado can spin at more than 300 miles an hour.

volcano (page 12)
An opening in Earth's surface through which magma erupts
Magma from a volcano can form ash, dust, and rock.

weathering (page 17)
The wearing away of rock over time
A canyon is created by weathering and fast-moving streams.

KEY CONCEPT

Index